Everybody Needs a Jay

Real Talk & Raw Truths From the Auntie You Never Knew You Needed

Jordynn James

This book is dedicated to promoting self-awareness, personal empowerment, and emotional healing. However, it is not intended as a substitute for professional medical or psychological advice. Readers experiencing severe emotional distress are encouraged to seek support from qualified healthcare professionals.

Table of Contents

Dedication

To my daughters—my greatest loves, my reason, my legacy. You are my heart walking in human form, my most divine creations. Every lesson I've learned, every trial I've overcome, was so I could pour wisdom into you. May you always know your worth, walk in your power, and never let this world silence you. Your voices are strong, your dreams are valid, and your existence alone is magic.

To my village—y'all held me up when I couldn't stand, reminded me who I was when I forgot, and never let me settle for less than I deserved. Thank you for seeing me, hearing me, and pushing me forward even when I swore, I was done. Your love is the foundation beneath my feet.

To my loved ones—you made me realize that my voice matters. You helped me see my story, struggles, and triumphs *mean something*. This book is for you and for every soul who stumbles across these pages. If even one word here makes your day a little brighter, your heart a little lighter, or your journey a little smoother—then I've done what I came here to do.

With all my love, "J."

"I wrote this book because I knew it was time. Time to do the work I was called to do. Time to take all the wisdom, the lessons, the trials, and the triumphs and share them with the world. It took me 45 years to get here, and it's been one hell of a ride. But one thing's for sure, and two things are for certain—I know what it feels like to be stuck, to question your worth, to wonder if you'll ever rise from what tried to break you. But I also know what it means to heal, to level up, and to step into the life you were meant to have."

Prologue

I've always felt like I was built different. Even as a kid, I wasn't the one flipping off the monkey bars or playing tag until my lungs burned. I was the one sitting on the bench, deep in conversation with my teachers, soaking up knowledge like a sponge. While my classmates were running wild at recess, I was busy talking about life, asking questions way beyond my years. Looking back, I realized that I wasn't just mature for my age, I was already stepping into the role I'd carry for most of my life.

I was *the* go-to". The problem-solver. The one people turned to when their world was falling apart. Whether it was my friends, my family, or the kids in the neighborhood, I somehow became everybody's mom. Not in the strict, do-your-homework kind of way, but in the way that made people feel safe. I was the cool one—the one who would listen without judging, who would tell you the truth even when it hurts, and who would wipe your tears while giving you a plan to fix your situation.

But what happens when the strong friend needs strength? What happens when *I'm* the one breaking? See, for all the advice I gave out, life made sure I had my own lessons to learn. And baby, let me tell you—*they came hard and fast*. I've had my heart shattered, my trust betrayed, and my world flipped upside down more times than I care to count.

I've been knocked down so many times I lost track. But here's the thing—I never stayed down. I had to learn how to take all the drama, all the heartbreaks, all the setbacks, and *find the lesson in them*. I had to stop seeing my struggles as punishments and start recognizing them as preparation. Because even in the ugliest, darkest moments, there was always something valuable waiting to be uncovered.

And that's why this book exists.

This isn't just a collection of words—it's a collection of *lessons*. It's proof that no matter how messy life gets, **you are still worthy.** Worthy of love, of happiness, of peace, of success. Even when you feel like you're at your lowest, like you have nothing left to give, like the weight of the world is pressing on your chest, you are still *enough*.

So, if you've ever felt lost, if you've ever questioned your worth, if you've ever needed a reminder that you *can* get back up, this book is for you. I hope that somewhere in these pages, you find a piece of yourself. A reason to keep pushing. A moment that makes you say, *Damn, I needed that.*

Because no matter where you've been or what you've been through, your story isn't over. You are not what you lost, you are not your mistakes, and you are **certainly** not defined by the people who didn't see your value.

So, take what you need from these pages, and remember—every lesson, every struggle, every tear you've cried was never in vain. You are still standing. You are still worthy. And trust me, your best days are still ahead of you.

Introduction

Life has a way of making sure you get the lesson, whether you're ready for it or not. I know that firsthand. I've lived, I've learned, and I've had to unlearn a whole lot along the way. This book? It's not just words on a page—it's a reflection of that journey.

I didn't always have the answers. Hell, sometimes I didn't even know the right questions to ask. But through every setback, every misstep, and every hard-earned win, I kept going. And that's why I'm here now—because I know I'm not the only one who's had to fight to find their way.

This isn't a book full of fluff and sugar-coated advice. It's real. It's raw. It's everything I wish someone would've told me when I was out here figuring it all out on my own. My life has been a mix of survival and self-discovery, of breaking cycles and building something better. I've been the one who gave too much, the one who poured into others before pouring into myself. I've outgrown spaces, outgrown people, and at times, outgrown the version of me that I once thought I had to be.

So, if you're ready for honesty, for accountability, and for the kind of insight that comes from lived experience, then you're in the right place. This book is for those who know they're meant for more but might need a push to step into it. It's for the ones who are tired of playing small, tired of settling, and ready to tap into their power.

Consider this your wake-up call. Your reminder that you are capable, worthy, and built for whatever is ahead. You don't have to have it all figured out today. You just have to be willing to do the work. And trust me—when you do, everything changes.

Let's Get Into It…

Chapter 1

Watch Your Mouth: The Power of Intentional Words and Protecting Your Peace

The *Good Book* tells us, *"Death and life are in the power of the tongue."* That means what we say—out loud, in our heads, in conversation with others—carries real weight. Words create energy, and that energy manifests in our lives whether we realize it or not. The universe doesn't process sarcasm, jokes, or casual negativity the way we do. It doesn't differentiate between *"I'm so tired of this life"* as a complaint versus a real declaration. It simply listens and delivers accordingly.

We don't always think about the way our words shape our reality, but they do. Think about it: How many times have you said something like, *"I'm broke," "My money is funny,"* or *"I can't catch a break"*? You might've meant it lightly, but the universe doesn't take it that way. It moves based on the energy you put out. You're telling it what to bring you more of—struggle, lack, and frustration.

Instead of speaking in lack, shift your words to expectation. Instead of *"I'm broke,"* say, *"The money is on the way."* Instead of *"I'm always tired,"* say, *"I'm restoring my energy."* Instead of *"I can't win for losing,"* say, *"Things are always working out in my favor."* Words are like seeds, and your life is the soil. What you plant will grow, whether it's weeds or wildflowers.

But it's not just about what *you* say, it's also about what you receive.

The Power of What You Hear and Receive

It's not enough to watch what you say; you also have to be intentional about what you allow yourself to hear. Words are powerful, whether they come from your own mouth or from someone else's. We've all got that *one* friend—the one who's always going through something, always in chaos, always in drama. You pick up the phone, and before you can even say *"Hey, how are you?"* they're already unloading:

"Girl, let me tell you what happened…"

You listen because you care. You let them vent, you try to offer advice, you try to help them see a way out of their mess. But by the time that call is over, you're *exhausted*.

Your mood has shifted. Your energy is low. You were fine before that conversation, but now, you're carrying the weight of someone else's problems.

Here's the thing: it's okay to care. But you can't care *more* than the person who actually has the problem. There's a difference between supporting someone and allowing their burdens to become yours. If you invest too much in someone else's drama, you might find yourself taking on energy that was never meant for you.

Think of it this way: Imagine someone walking around with a heavy backpack full of rocks. They keep complaining about how heavy it is, how it's slowing them down, how it's ruining their life. But when you offer to help them take the rocks out, they refuse.

They just want to talk about how heavy the bag is. Now, if you stand there long enough, one of two things will happen: you'll either take the bag from them and carry it yourself, or you'll walk away drained just from standing next to all that weight.

Neither of those options is good for you.

It's important to protect your peace. That doesn't mean you stop being a good friend or that you stop caring about people. It means you recognize your limits. If someone is constantly in chaos and never taking steps to change their situation, you have to ask yourself: *Is this a conversation I need to be a part of?* Is this adding anything to my life, or is it only draining me?

Why Protecting Your Energy Matters

Energy is real. The people you surround yourself with, the conversations you engage in, and the words you allow into your space all impact you more than you think. If you're constantly surrounded by negativity—whether it's your own or someone else's—you're going to feel weighed down. You might not even realize why, but you'll notice things just feel *off*.

This is why it's crucial to be intentional not just about what you *say*, but what you *listen to*. Surround yourself with conversations that are edifying to your soul. Engage with people who uplift you, inspire you, and encourage you to grow. That doesn't mean you ignore problems or pretend life is perfect, but it does mean you're mindful about where you place your energy.

There's also a deeper spiritual aspect to all of this. When you constantly engage in other people's drama, you risk taking on karma that isn't even yours. Imagine you getting too involved in someone else's mess. If you keep trying to fix things for them, if you take on their battles as your own, you might find yourself suffering consequences that were never meant for you.

Have you ever noticed how some people always seem to be in the middle of something, even when it has nothing to do with them? That's because they've invested in problems that weren't theirs to begin with. You have to be mindful of the energy you pick up.

How to Be More Intentional with Your Words and Energy

1. **Speak Life** – Every time you catch yourself speaking negatively, reframe it. Instead of *"I never*

get what I want," say, *"Everything that's meant for me is making its way to me."* Instead of *"I'm failing,"* say, *"I'm learning and growing."*

2. **Set Boundaries** – It's okay to love people from a distance. If someone's conversations are always draining, set limits on how much time you spend engaging in them.

3. **Be Mindful of Media** – What you consume matters. If you're constantly listening to sad music, watching toxic reality TV, or scrolling through negative social media posts, that energy is seeping into you. Balance it with content that lifts you.

4. **Check Your Circle** – Are the people around you adding to your life or draining it? Are your conversations mostly about growth and solutions, or are they just endless cycles of complaining? Surround yourself with people who challenge you to be better.

5. **Trust the Process** – Change doesn't happen overnight, but the more you practice intentional speaking and mindful listening, and the more you'll see the shift. At the end of the day, words are powerful, and energy is real. What you say and what you allow into your space will shape your reality. So be intentional. Be mindful. And most importantly, protect your peace.

Chapter 2

When Love Is a Lie: The Truth About Soul Ties & Trauma Bonds

"They said it plain before: love has a way of clowning you. One minute it's butterflies, the next it's migraines. You're left asking yourself, *if this isn't love, then why does it live in my chest rent-free? Why does it ache, but still keep me coming back for more?*"

You know, just like I do, that love should be none of those things if you've been following along. But here we are, decades later, still thinking it's just a song about heartbreak when really, it's a whole revelation wrapped in melody. Because love—real love— doesn't have you questioning your sanity or running in circles trying to justify pain. Yet, we find ourselves tangled up in connections that feel all-consuming, only to realize too late that it wasn't "love" at all.

Soul ties and trauma bonds—two chains that can feel eerily like love but are anything but. A soul tie is that deep, unshakable connection with another person, a fusion of

6

emotions, thoughts, and energies that can either elevate or drain you. When formed with the wrong person, it becomes a binding contract with chaos. Imagine pouring your entire spirit into someone who only mirrors back your insecurities, leaving you addicted to a toxic cycle of highs and lows. That's not love—that's spiritual entrapment.

Trauma bonds, on the other hand, are the psychological trickery that keeps us attached to pain, mistaking it for passion. They develop in abusive or toxic relationships where moments of affection are weaponized to keep you hooked. Your brain starts to crave those rare "good times" like a drug, convincing you to endure the bad just for another hit of what you once thought was love. Psychologists call it intermittent reinforcement—a manipulation tactic that keeps you trapped. According to research by Carnes (2019), trauma bonds function similarly to addiction, releasing dopamine and oxytocin in response to both love and mistreatment, making it incredibly difficult to walk away.

How to Spot Soul Ties & Trauma Bonds

Not every strong connection is a soul tie, and not every deep attachment is a trauma bond. The difference lies in how it affects your well-being. Here's how to recognize when you're entangled in something unhealthy:

- **You can't stop thinking about them—even when they've hurt you.** Your mind replays the good times, making excuses for the bad.

- **Your identity feels wrapped up in them.** You struggle to see who you are outside of the relationship.

- **You feel drained instead of fulfilled.** The connection demands more than it gives, leaving you emotionally exhausted.

- **You justify red flags.** You convince yourself that mistreatment is love, or that their pain excuses their behavior.

- **You feel withdrawal when they pull away.** Just like addiction, you crave their presence, even if it's toxic.

Breaking Free: The Hardest, Best Thing You'll Ever Do

Letting go of a soul tie or trauma bond isn't easy, but it's necessary for your growth. Walking away feels like ripping out a part of yourself, but in reality, you're reclaiming what was always yours—your peace, your clarity, your power. Psychologists suggest that healing requires breaking the cycle of intermittent reinforcement, which means resisting the urge to return when the "good moments" come back around (Carnes, 2019).

Healing starts with **acknowledgment**—understanding that love should never feel like suffering. Then comes **detoxing**—physically, emotionally, and spiritually removing them from your life. That means blocking, deleting, and refusing to entertain their energy.

Rebuilding yourself is the final step—rediscovering your own identity and learning what love should actually look like.

Yes, it's painful. Yes, you'll grieve. But what's on the other side? Freedom. Self-respect. The ability to welcome a love that doesn't make you second-guess your worth.

Misery loves company because it needs someone to commiserate with. But you? You were meant to rise. You were meant to heal. And most importantly, you were meant to experience love that doesn't hurt.

Chapter 3

Self-Care: Because When You Look Good, You Feel Good

Let's get one thing straight—self-care is *not* selfish. It's survival. It's maintenance. It's standing in the mirror, looking at your fine self, and saying, *"Yeah, I did that."* Because when you look good, you feel good, and when you feel good, you move differently.

Self-care is not just bubble baths and spa days (Now, don't get it twisted—those count too). It's about showing up for *you* the way you show up for everyone else. It's about refusing to let yourself become the last thing on your own priority list. Because let's be real, you can't pour from an empty cup—and you *sure* can't pour from one that's cracked, chipped, and begging for a refill.

The Wake-Up Call: When I Realized I Was Running on Empty

There was a time when I thought "grinding" meant putting *everything* ahead of me. Work, people, responsibilities—*all* of it. If there was something to be done, I was doing it. And self-care? That was a luxury I didn't have time for.

But then one day, I caught a glimpse of myself in the mirror, and I didn't even recognize the woman looking back. She was tired. She was drained. And worst of all? She looked like she had *given up on herself.*

That was the moment I knew something had to change. Because I realized that *when I don't take care of myself, it shows.* It shows in my energy. It shows in my attitude. It shows in the way I carry myself. And if I'm walking around feeling like I just survived an apocalypse, how can I expect to manifest blessings, opportunities, or even a decent mood?

Self-Care Is an Obligation, Not a Luxury

Society will have you thinking that taking care of yourself is "extra." Doing your hair, putting on a little gloss, or taking time to just breathe is something you have to *earn.* But let me tell you something—self-care is not a reward. It's not a privilege. **It's a necessity.**

- Self-care is choosing *you* in a world that benefits from you being exhausted.

- Self-care is looking in the mirror and saying, *"Damn, I look good today,"* and *meaning* it.

- Self-care is not waiting until you're burned out to give yourself the grace you give to everybody else.

Because let's be honest—when you feel like trash, everything around you starts feeling like trash, too. But when you feel good, when you *invest* in yourself, you step differently. You speak differently. You attract *better*.

Look Good, Feel Good, Move Like You Deserve More

Listen, I'm not saying you need to be done up every single day. But I *am* saying that letting yourself go is not an act of humility; it's an act of neglect. There is power in showing up for yourself, even in the smallest ways.

- You ever noticed how different your energy is when your hair is fresh? When your skin is glowing? When you throw on that outfit that hugs you in *all* the right places?

- You ever catch your reflection when you're feeling yourself and think, *"Oh, I really am that girl"*?

- You ever take the time to just sit in stillness, breathe deep, and remember that you are not a machine— that you deserve *care*, too?

That's the power of self-care. It *re-centers* you. It *rebuilds* you. It reminds you that you are not just a workhorse, not just a problem solver, not someone holding everything together for everyone else.

You are *you*. And that is worth taking care of.

Excuses Won't Love You Back

Now, I know some of y'all are reading this thinking, *"But I don't have time for self-care."* Let me stop you right there. You have time for what you make time for. And if you can make time for work, for drama, for scrolling mindlessly on your phone, you can make time for *yourself*.

Excuses won't love you back. That job? It will replace you in a week. That stressful situation? It will still be there after you take 30 minutes to do something for *yourself*. That to-do list? It will never be done—so stop waiting for the "perfect" moment to prioritize yourself.

If you don't put yourself on your schedule, who will?

The Ultimate Flex: Being Unapologetic About You

Let's be clear, taking care of yourself is not just about looking good for other people. It's about *feeling* good for *you*. It's about knowing that when you show up in a room, your energy introduces you before you even speak. It's about recognizing that *you* are the main character in your own life.

So, whether it's a skincare routine, a fresh set, journaling, sitting in silence, or simply saying *no* when you're tired—do it *without guilt*. Take the time. Make the effort. Stand in the mirror and remind yourself that you are worth it.

Because the best version of you? *It only happens when you choose to take care of yourself.*

Chapter 4

Fix Ya Crown! Stop Acting Small...
(SELF-WORTH & SELF-LOVE)

For the longest time, I thought enduring was strength. I thought if I could just hold on, if I could just love him enough, if I could just be *better*, things would change. I became a master at surviving, at making excuses for the pain, at convincing myself that it wasn't *that* bad.

But the truth? **I was shrinking.**

Piece by piece, I was disappearing.

I wasn't laughing the way I used to. My voice, once loud and full of life, had become hesitant, careful, afraid to set him off. The things that made me, *me*. My joy, my confidence, my dreams—felt like distant memories. I was still breathing, still functioning, still showing up, but I wasn't *living*. I was existing in a space that was slowly swallowing me whole.

I had forgotten who I was.

That realization didn't hit me all at once. It came in whispers, in small moments where I caught a glimpse of the woman I used to be. A joke I stopped myself from laughing too loud at. An outfit I once would have worn with confidence, but now second-guess. A dream I had abandoned because he convinced me it wasn't realistic.

I had become a shell of myself.

And that's when I knew—*enduring wasn't strength.* Strength was remembering **who the hell I was.**

It didn't happen overnight. Rebuilding takes time. I had to stop, take a deep breath, and start undoing the damage. I had to remind myself that this situation, this pain, **did not define me.** I was not weak for loving, for hoping, for trying. And I was *not* broken just because someone else didn't see my worth.

I started speaking life back into myself.

I started reclaiming the things I had lost—my laughter, my confidence, my power. I stopped shrinking. I stopped making myself small to fit into spaces that weren't meant for me. And most importantly, I stopped *enduring* just for the sake of surviving.

I was meant to thrive.

So, if you're reading this and you feel like you've been fading, like you've lost yourself somewhere along the way, **this is your reminder:** You are not what hurt you. You are not what you survived. **You are still you.** Underneath all the pain, all the doubt, all the years of making yourself small, *you are still you.*

Fix ya crown, sis. **Remember who you are.** And never let this world make you forget again.

Let's get one thing straight: **You are the prize.** Period. Not an option, not a backup plan, and certainly not something to be played with. Too many times, we dim our light to make others comfortable, or worse, wait for someone else to tell us we shine. That stops today.

This section is all about reminding you who you are and what you bring to the table. If you've ever questioned your worth, felt unappreciated, or settled for less than you deserve, then these affirmations are for you. You're about to step into a new era where self-doubt has no room, confidence is your daily vibe, and self-love isn't an option—it's mandatory.

Stop looking for validation in people who can't even validate their own parking. **The way you love yourself sets the standard for how the world loves you back.** So, if you're not treating yourself like royalty, how can you expect anyone else to?

It's time to reclaim your power. Adjust your crown, step into your greatness, and remember: **You set the standard. They either rise to meet it or get left behind. So, the next time you're in your head about your value, here are some affirmations to help remind you just who the Eff you are.**

"You are the prize, act accordingly."

Stop letting people treat you like a clearance sale. Walk like you're designer, think like you're luxury, and know you're worth every penny.

"If they can't match your energy, they don't deserve your presence."

Stop dimming your light to make other people comfortable. Shine regardless—if they can't handle it, let them find shade somewhere else.

"I validate me. Period."

Waiting for other people's approval will leave you empty. Love yourself first, and the right people will show up to celebrate you.

"I will not beg for love, respect, or reciprocity."

Anything you have to beg for isn't worth having. Walk away from anything that requires you to shrink to fit.

"I am my own standard."

Stop competing with people who don't even know where they're going. Be better than the person you were yesterday; that's the only competition that matters.

"I was never 'too much'—they were just never enough."

Stop apologizing for your confidence, your ambition, or your energy. You're not "too much"; they just weren't enough for you.

"My peace is non-negotiable."

*If it costs you your peace, it's too expensive. Protect your energy
like it's your most valuable asset—because it is.*

"I will not shrink to fit someone else's expectations."

**You were never meant to fit in. You were meant to stand out.
Be bold, be loud, be you.*

**"I love myself loudly, proudly,
and without hesitation."**

*Self-love ain't selfish. The way you love yourself sets the standard
for how others love you.*

"I became the person I needed when I was younger."

*Heal. Grow. Be the version of you that your younger self
would be proud of.*

Chapter 5

The Gratitude Mindset: You Get More When You Appreciate the Little Things

Gratitude is a game-changer. It's the difference between feeling like life is working *for* you instead of constantly working *against* you. It's that little shift in perspective that turns "I *have* to" into "I *get* to." And let me tell you—when you start moving in gratitude, life starts moving for you.

See, people love to wait until the "big" blessings roll in before they express appreciation. They want to hit the jackpot, get the promotion, find the love of their life, and *then* they'll be thankful. But let's talk about what happens when you learn to be grateful *before* the breakthrough—because *that* is the secret sauce.

Gratitude Unlocks More

The universe is like a generous but very observant friend. It watches how you treat what you *already* have before it decides to give you more. You ever noticed how some people always seem to be attracting blessings left and right? It's not because they're lucky. It's because they *already* know how to celebrate the little things.

- They don't just wait for a raise to be grateful—they're thankful for the job they *already* have.

- They don't just wait for the perfect house—they appreciate the roof over their head *now*.

- They don't just wait for the big love story—they cherish the relationships *they do* have, whether it's friends, family, or themselves.

And because they already move in gratitude, they stay in a state of *receiving*. Meanwhile, the people who constantly complain, who never acknowledge the good in their lives, stay stuck. Because why would life give you more when you don't even appreciate what's in front of you?

A Thankful Heart Is a Magnet for More

Let's be real—nobody wants to keep giving to someone who never says thank you. Imagine constantly doing favors for someone, showing up for them, giving them gifts, and they *never* acknowledge it. At some point, you'd stop, right?

Now, apply that to life. If you keep overlooking your blessings, if you keep acting like nothing is ever *enough*, why would life keep sending you more?

Gratitude is not just about *saying* thank you, it's about *feeling* it. It's about waking up and recognizing that even on your worst days, there's *something* to be grateful for.

- The fact that you woke up? That's a gift.

- The fact that you have a phone, Wi-Fi, and the ability to read this right now? That's a blessing.

- The fact that you have even *one* person in your life who loves you? That's a reason to be thankful. When you start acknowledging the small things, the universe takes notice. And before you know it, you'll start attracting bigger and better opportunities— simply because you made space for them with gratitude.

The Trap of "Never Enough" Thinking

Some people stay in a constant state of *lack*—not because they don't have enough, but because they refuse to recognize what they *do* have. They're always chasing the next thing, always waiting for *more* before they allow themselves to feel happy.

- "I'll be happy when I make six figures."

- "I'll feel successful when I buy a house."

- "I'll finally feel good about myself when I lose weight."

The problem with this mindset? **You'll always be chasing.** Because the moment you reach one goal, you'll just replace it with another. And that finish line you keep running toward? It *keeps moving.*

Gratitude is what allows you to *enjoy* life while you're still in the process. It's what keeps you from looking back years later and realizing you never actually *lived*—you were just *waiting.*

Your Words Set the Tone for Your Life

Let's talk about the power of your words. Because just like self-care, gratitude isn't just about what you *do*, it's about how you *speak.* If you're constantly talking about what's wrong, what's missing, what's *not* happening for you, then guess what? That's exactly what you're going to experience more of.

But when you start flipping the script? When you replace complaints with appreciation? Everything shifts. *(See how intentional speaking fits in here? I know... say less.)*

- Instead of saying, *"I'm broke,"* say, *"Money is on the way."*

- Instead of saying, *"Nothing good ever happens to me,"* say, *"I attract good things effortlessly."*

- Instead of saying, *"I hate my job,"* say, *"This job is a stepping stone to something greater."*

Remember—the universe doesn't understand sarcasm. If you're constantly saying negative things, even as a joke, that's what you're programming your reality to reflect.

Your words shape your world. So, speak gratitude, and watch your world change.

Gratitude Protects Your Peace

Being grateful doesn't mean ignoring the tough stuff. It doesn't mean pretending life is perfect when it's not. What it *does* mean is choosing to focus on what's *right* instead of obsessing over what's wrong. See, there's a blessing in everything, good or bad. You just have to find it.

Have you ever had a conversation with someone who *only* talks about their problems? You get on the phone with them, and before you even say "hello," they're already dumping all their drama on you? And by the time you hang up, you feel *drained*—like they just transferred all their bad energy onto you?

That's what happens when you surround yourself with people who *reject* gratitude. Their energy pulls you down. Their words fill your mind with negativity. And before you know it, *you're* feeling miserable, too.

This is why protecting your peace is essential. Because no matter how much you love someone, you *cannot* let them drag you into their storm.

- It's okay to care—but you can't care *more* than the person with the problem.

- It's okay to listen—but don't absorb what isn't yours to carry.

- It's okay to help—but don't invest so deeply that you end up suffering for something that had *nothing* to do with you in the first place.

You don't owe anyone a front-row seat to your energy if they're only going to fill your space with complaints and chaos. Boundaries are love, too.

Gratitude Is the Ultimate Cheat Code

At the end of the day, gratitude is not just about being polite. It's a strategy. It's a mindset. It's the ultimate cheat code to a more joyful, abundant life.

Because when you truly start *living* in gratitude:

- You stop chasing happiness, you start *experiencing* it.

- You stop focusing on what's missing, you start *appreciating* what's here.

- You stop blocking your blessings, you start *inviting* more of them in.

So, if you're waiting for a sign to shift your perspective, this is it. Start with what you have. Appreciate what's in front of you. Speak life into your reality.

Because when you master the gratitude mindset, you'll realize—**you were never lacking. You were just overlooking your abundance.**

Chapter 6

"Get This Money & Claim Your Blessings"

(MANIFESTING ABUNDANCE & SUCCESS)

Get This Money & Claim Your Blessings

For the longest time, I moved like money was something that happened to *other* people. Not me. I played it safe, worked hard, followed the rules, and still found myself stuck— counting dollars before payday, stretching meals, saying "next time" to things I deserved *now*.

I had been taught to survive, not thrive.

See, growing up, I heard all the usual lines: *"Money doesn't grow on trees." "You gotta work twice as hard to have half as much." "Be grateful for what you got."* And while there's wisdom in gratitude and hard work, what I didn't realize was that **I was playing small.** I was thinking small. I was putting limits on myself before life even had a chance to.

That had to stop.

I had to stop seeing wealth as something out of reach. I had to stop treating money like a struggle and start treating it like a tool—like something that was *already mine*, just waiting for me to step up and claim it.

I started shifting my mindset.

I started saying, *"Money flows to me effortlessly."* Even when my account said otherwise. I stopped feeling guilty about wanting abundance. **Because why wouldn't I want more?** More peace. More success. More *options*.

And when I tell you the doors started opening? Baby, they *flew* open. Hell, it damn near scared me.

Not because I wished for it. Not because I sat around manifesting without action. But because I finally moved like someone who deserved it. I started investing in myself, in my growth, in my craft. I stopped saying "I can't afford it" and started asking, *"How can I afford it?"* I stopped waiting for permission and started **walking like the money already belonged to me.**

And it did.

Because here's the truth: *Money is energy. Success is energy. And when you start moving like you're worthy of it, it will chase you down.*

So, if you've been playing small, waiting for your turn, or second-guessing your ability to step into abundance,

stop that right now. Fix your mindset, fix your grind, and **claim your blessings.**

This world has more than enough. The money, the success, the opportunities—they're already out there. **So why not you?**

Go get it. **It's already yours.**

Abundance isn't just about money—it's about a *mindset*. Too many people walk around with a "broke" mentality, thinking success is only for the lucky, the privileged, or the people who were "born into it." Nah. **Success is for those who claim it, believe in it, and work for it.**

If you've been doubting your ability to attract wealth, happiness, or success, consider this your wake-up call. The energy you put out is the energy that comes back, so if you're constantly speaking lack, struggle, and stress into existence—guess what?

That's what's gonna show up.

These affirmations will help you shift that thinking. You're about to start walking like money, talking like prosperity, and **manifesting like a boss**. The universe is listening— so make sure you're saying something worth receiving.

No more "I hope I get this." From now on, it's "This is MINE."

Get in the mirror and use these as your reminder...

"Money flows to me effortlessly, and I receive it with gratitude."

Stop stressing about what you don't have—abundance starts with a mindset. Walk like it's already yours.

"I am a magnet for success, opportunities, and prosperity."

What you attract starts with what you believe. Speak it, expect it, and watch how the universe delivers.

"My hustle and my faith will always provide."

You weren't made to struggle forever. Work hard, believe harder, and trust that everything is falling into place.

"Opportunities chase me down because I am prepared for them."

Success ain't about luck; it's about being ready when your moment comes. Stay ready, so you never have to get ready.

"I release all doubt and claim the life I deserve."

You can't manifest abundance while holding onto fear. Let it go, and let the blessings roll in.

"I don't chase; I attract. What's meant for me will always find me."

Stop forcing what's not flowing. What's truly for you will never require you to beg, chase, or compromise your worth.

"Wealth is my birthright, and I claim it now."

Change your mindset about money. You were not born to struggle—speak abundance and claim it.

"I walk in rooms like I belong there, because I do."

Stop doubting yourself. You earned your seat at the table—now act like it.

"Every dollar I spend comes back to me multiplied."

Shift from a scarcity mindset to an abundance mindset. There's more where that came from.

"I deserve every blessing coming my way."

*Stop questioning your worth. You are deserving, you are capable, and you are *ready*.

Chapter 7

"Hustle, Heal & Handle Your Business"
(MOTIVATION & DRIVE)

Hustle, Heal & Handle Your Business

Nobody ever tells you how hard it is to do *both*—to chase your dreams while picking up the broken pieces of yourself at the same time. To keep pushing forward when life keeps throwing you setbacks. To hustle for your future while healing from your past.

But let me tell you something: **You can do both.**

For a long time, I thought I had to wait until I felt *whole* before I could really go after what I wanted. I thought I had to have all my trauma neatly packed away, my heart fully mended, my spirit unshaken, before I could step into my blessings. But the truth?

Healing is an ongoing process, and life doesn't wait for you to be ready.

So I had to learn how to move through it.

I had to learn how to hustle even when my heart was heavy. I had to learn how to put my energy into something bigger than my pain. And I had to learn that healing isn't about sitting still and waiting—it's about actively *choosing* yourself every single day.

Some days, that meant grinding hard, securing the bag, and making the most out of my ambitions. Other days, it meant giving myself grace, letting myself cry, and knowing that rest was just as important as the work.

And the key? **Balance.**

You don't have to choose between success and self-care. You don't have to choose between ambition and emotional well-being. **You are allowed to build your empire while healing your soul.**

So, sis—don't think you have to be perfect before you go after what's yours. Hustle, heal, and handle your business. **You are capable of doing all three.**

Let's be real—motivationreal, motivation is cute, but **discipline** is what gets results. Some days, you'll feel like getting up and chasing your dreams. Other days, you won't even wanna roll outta bed. But here's the secret: **You gotta move, whether you feel like it or not.**

This section is for those moments when you're ready to give up, when the grind feels pointless, or when you start believing success is "too far away." The truth? **It's only far if you stop moving.**

Excuses don't make money. Hustle does. These affirmations will remind you that every small step forward is progress, that consistency is the real key to success, and that **you're capable of more than you think.**

Stay hungry. Stay focused. And remember—**every boss was once a beginner; every empire started with a single move.** Let this be yours.

These are the cardinal rules:

"Excuses don't make money."

You can have excuses, or you can have results—but you can't have both.

"I don't wait for opportunities, I create them."

*You are the CEO of your own life. Stop waiting for permission and *go get it.*

"Discipline will take you where motivation won't."

Some days you won't feel like it—do it anyway. That's how winners move.

"Hustle in silence; let success make the noise."

Move like a boss, not a broadcaster. Let your work do the talking.

"Nobody's coming to save you. Be your own hero."

It's on you. Get up, handle your business, and stop waiting for someone to rescue you.

"Stay humble, but never stay quiet."

Humility doesn't mean silence. Speak up, claim your space, and own your greatness.

"Your comfort zone is where dreams go to die."

If it doesn't challenge you, it doesn't change you. Step up.

"I refuse to be the same person next year."

Growth is mandatory. Evolve, level up, and let them be mad.

"I grind now so I can flex later."

Sacrifice today for the life you want tomorrow.

"The best revenge is success."

Don't get even—get better, get richer, and get so happy they can't stand it.

Chapter 8

Accountability: The Mirror You Can't Afford to Avoid

A ccountability is a word people love to throw around but hate to apply to themselves. It's easy to talk about how other people need to take responsibility for their actions, but when it's time to turn that mirror on ourselves? That's where most folks tap out. The truth is, accountability isn't just about admitting when you're wrong—it's about owning your role in your life. It's about recognizing that your choices, your reactions, and even your inaction all play a part in where you are today.

And let's be real—dodging accountability might feel good in the moment, but it's a guaranteed way to stay stuck. If you never take responsibility for your part in things, you'll keep repeating the same mistakes, running into the same walls, and wondering why life isn't changing for you. Accountability isn't a punishment—it's the key to your own growth.

The Day I Realized I Was in My Own Way

I had this habit of thinking that if something went wrong in my relationships— friendships, family, business— it was because of *them*. They weren't listening, they weren't being fair, they weren't understanding where I was coming from. And while, yes, sometimes people *do* move foul, I had to have a real moment with myself: *What if I'm the common denominator?*

I remember a specific situation that hit me hard. There was a falling out with someone close to me, and for the longest time, I told myself the narrative that made me feel better: *They did me wrong. They should've handled things differently. They should've known how I felt without me having to say it.*

But here's the thing about accountability—it forces you to stop living in your feelings and start dealing with facts. And the fact was, I wasn't communicating properly. I was expecting people to read my mind. I was reacting instead of responding. I was playing victim in situations where I actually had control but chose not to exercise it.

And once I really sat with that truth, I had to laugh at myself. How was I mad at people for not understanding my needs when I hadn't even articulated them properly? How was I holding grudges over things that could've been resolved with one real conversation?

The Freedom That Comes with Owning Your Part

Here's what they don't tell you—accountability makes life *easier*. Yes, it stings at first. Nobody enjoys admitting they were wrong or that they contributed to their own mess. But once you start practicing it, you realize how much weight you've been carrying by blaming everything outside of yourself.

When you take accountability, you take your power back. If you acknowledge that you played a role in a problem, that means you also have the power to *change* it. That's real freedom.

Think about it: If every bad situation in your life is someone else's fault, you're basically saying you have no control over your own life. You're just a passenger, hoping the people around you drive carefully. But when you take responsibility, you move to the driver's seat. You get to decide how you move forward.

The Downside of Avoiding Accountability

Now, let's talk about what happens when you *don't* take accountability. Because let's be honest—avoiding it is tempting. Nobody wants to sit down and dissect their own flaws. It's much easier to blame other people, circumstances, bad luck, or the alignment of the planets.

But here's what dodging accountability *really* gets you:

1. **The Same Problems on Repeat** – If you don't acknowledge your role in your issues, you'll keep running into the same situations over and over. Different people, different settings, but the *same* conflict.

2. **Strained Relationships** – People don't respect someone who never owns up to their mistakes. If you're always deflecting, blaming, or playing the victim, after a while, folks stop engaging. Nobody wants to be in a one-sided dynamic where they're always the villain in *your* story.

3. **Limited Growth** – The biggest downside? You stay stagnant. When you refuse to see where you could improve, you cheat yourself out of personal development.

Edgy Truths About Accountability

- If life keeps handing you the same lesson, maybe the test ain't over because you keep failing it.

- Nobody owes you understanding if you refuse to communicate.

- If you refuse to acknowledge your flaws, you'll keep attracting people who expose them.

- Growth is uncomfortable, but so is staying the same. Pick your pain.

How Accountability Transforms Your Relationships

Once I started taking accountability, my relationships changed *fast*. Conversations that used to turn into arguments became actual discussions. Instead of getting defensive, I learned to listen—really *listen*—to what people were telling me. And instead of assuming I was always right, I started asking myself: *What can I do differently?*

That's not to say that everyone in my life magically became perfect—far from it. But once I started focusing on what *I* could control, I stopped feeling so frustrated all the time. Instead of getting mad at people for not showing up the way I wanted them to, I got clear on my expectations and communicated them. Instead of holding grudges, I addressed problems as they came up.

And let me tell you, that level of self-awareness? It's a game-changer.

How to Start Taking Accountability

If you're ready to step into that level of growth, here's where to start:

1. **Check Your Patterns** – If you keep running into the same issues, take a step back. What's the common factor? (Hint: It's probably you.)

2. **Own Your Reactions** – You can't control what people do, but you *can* control how you respond. If your default is to lash out, shut down, or avoid the issue, that's something to work on.

3. **Apologize Without Excuses** – A real apology doesn't include the word *but*. Stop justifying, stop explaining, and just say *"I was wrong. I'll do better."*

4. **Ask for Feedback** – If you're serious about growth, ask the people closest to you, *"What's something I could improve on?"* And don't get mad at their answer.

5. **Commit to Change** – Accountability isn't a one-time thing. It's a daily practice. The goal isn't perfection—it's progress.

Final Thoughts: Accountability is a Gift

At the end of the day, accountability isn't about beating yourself up—it's about leveling up. It's about realizing that you *do* have control over your life, your relationships, and your future. And once you embrace that? Everything changes.

The mirror might be uncomfortable, but trust me—it's worth looking into. Because on the other side of accountability is peace, growth, and a life that actually feels good to live.

Chapter 9

"Drop the Baggage & Level Up"
(Healing & Letting Go)

Drop the Baggage & Level Up

For the longest time, I held on to my pain like it was some kind of armor. Like staying mad, staying hurt, staying *ready* was gonna protect me from ever being played again. I convinced myself that holding a grudge gave me power, that replaying the betrayals in my mind somehow kept me in control.

But all it did was keep me *stuck*.

I spent so much time thinking about what they did to me, how unfair it was, how I deserved better. And in doing that, I let them take up space in my mind, in my heart, in my *future*. I was so focused on *them* that I forgot about *myself*.

That's what self-sabotage looks like: holding onto something so tight that you can't grab what's next.

And then one day, it hit me: **forgiveness isn't about them. It's about me.**

But don't get it twisted, **forgiving doesn't mean forgetting.** Oh, I remember *exactly* what they did. I remember the lies, the betrayal, the way they took my kindness for weakness. But remembering doesn't mean I have to relive it. It doesn't mean I have to carry that pain like a badge of honor.

See, I used to think forgiving meant letting them off the hook, like I was saying what they did was okay. But nah— *forgiveness just meant I was done letting it control me.* It meant I was freeing up my energy for things that actually served me.

Because let's be real, karma doesn't need help. The universe is always watching, and what people put out, they *will* get back. That's not my job to worry about. My job? **To level up.** To move past the pain and into the life I *deserve.*

So, if you're still holding on to old hurt, still waiting on that "I'm sorry" that may never come, still replaying the past like it's gonna change—**let that go.**

Drop the baggage. It's too heavy to carry where you're going.

Listen—closure is cute, but **you don't need an apology to move on.** Some people are never going to say sorry, never gonna acknowledge the hurt they caused, and never gonna be who you needed them to be. And you know what? **That's their problem, not yours.**

Holding onto pain only keeps *you* stuck. Letting go isn't about them—it's about freeing yourself. You don't heal by replaying the past; you heal by **building a future so good that the past looks like a lesson, not a loss.**

If you've ever wasted energy on someone who wouldn't do the same for you, this section is your permission slip to **let that sh*t go.** Life is too short to carry dead weight, and **the best revenge is living well.**

What's the point in tripping over rocks in the rearview?

So read these affirmations, say them out loud, and step into your new era—**one where you're no longer waiting on closure, apologies, or old love to circle back.** You're **too busy winning** to look back now.

"Closure is a scam. Heal yourself and keep it moving."

Stop waiting for apologies that may never come.
You owe yourself peace.

"I don't waste time on people who wouldn't do the same for me."

Loyalty is a two-way street. If it ain't mutual, let it go.

"Some people are only in your life to teach you what you don't want."

Every experience is a lesson. Learn it, and move on.

"I forgive, but I don't forget. Lesson learned."

Forgiveness is for you. But remembering the lesson? That's for your future self.

"Their rejection was my redirection."

What you lost wasn't a loss. It was a setup for something better.

Chapter 10

Standing on Business: Boundaries, Balance, and Being About YOU

Let's talk about boundaries. Real boundaries. Not the half-hearted, "I guess I'll say no this time" type, but the kind that makes it *crystal clear* where you stand. The kind that protects your peace, your energy, and your self-respect.

Because here's the thing—if you don't set the tone for how people can treat you, they *will* decide for you. And let's be honest, some folks will test your limits just to see how much they can get away with. That's why standing on business—when it comes to *you*—is non-negotiable.

The Moment I Realized I Was Letting Too Much Slide

There was a time when I was the *yes* girl. The *'Sure, I got it'* friend. The *I'll figure it out* person—even when I had nothing left to give. And you know what that got me? Burnt out, frustrated, and secretly resenting the very people I was trying to help.

One day, after yet another long conversation where someone dumped their problems on me like I was a free therapist, I sat there drained. Not just tired—*soul exhausted.* And I had to ask myself: *Why do I keep allowing this?*

I realized that I wasn't just helping people—I was overextending myself to keep the peace. To avoid conflict. To be seen as reliable, dependable, "one of the real ones." But at what cost? My mental health? My own priorities? My *peace?*

And that's when it hit me—I wasn't standing on business when it came to *me.*

The Power of Boundaries: Why They Matter

We hear the word *boundaries* all the time, but let's break down what they *really* mean. Boundaries aren't about shutting people out or being selfish. They're about *self-respect.* They're about knowing your limits and not letting guilt, pressure, or manipulation push you past them.

Because let's be real—people will *always* ask for more. More time, more energy, more access. And if you don't put some structure in place, you'll wake up one day feeling completely depleted with nothing left for yourself.

So here's the truth:

- Boundaries are not mean. They're necessary.

- Saying "no" is a complete sentence.

- You don't owe anyone unlimited access to you.

- Your peace is more important than someone else's comfort.

What Happens When You Don't Stand on Business?

When you let people cross your boundaries, you teach them that your limits are optional. You train them to believe that you'll always bend, always be available, always put yourself last. And once people get used to that version of you? They will *expect* it.

- You become the go-to problem solver, even when you don't want to be.

- You find yourself drained from conversations that don't pour back into you.

- You start feeling resentment toward the very people you love.

- You lose sight of *your* needs because you're too busy catering to everyone else's.

And let's talk about that one friend—the one who's *always* going through something. Every time they call, it's a *crisis*. Every conversation leaves you feeling *heavier* than when you started. And you love them, so you keep answering, keep listening, keep absorbing all that negative energy.

But here's the thing: **you cannot keep pouring into someone who refuses to refill themselves.** You cannot be someone's emotional landfill. It is *not* your job to take on someone else's burdens so deeply that you end up carrying their karma.

Caring is beautiful, but caring *more than the person with the problem*? That's self-sacrifice. And that is not standing on business.

How I Started Protecting My Peace

Once I realized I had been betraying myself in the name of "being a good person," I made a decision—I was done. Done stretching myself thin. Done entertaining conversations that left me drained. Done feeling guilty for putting myself first.

And here's what I started doing differently:

1. I Stopped Explaining My No

I used to feel like I had to justify why I couldn't do something. But guess what? *I don't owe anybody a dissertation on why I'm choosing myself.* Now, when something doesn't align with me, I simply say, *"No, that doesn't work for me."* And I leave it at that.

2. I Limited My Availability

I started being intentional about *who* gets access to my energy. Not everyone deserves unlimited access to you. Some people only call when they need something. Some people only show up when it benefits them. I started recognizing the difference between *genuine connec*tions and *one-sided leeching.*

3. I Redirected Draining Conversations

Now, when that one friend starts spiraling into the same negativity, instead of letting it consume me, I say, *"What's the solution here?"* If they're just venting with no intention of changing the situation, I don't engage. Because at the end of the day, *some people don't want advice—they want an audience.* And I no longer sign up for that role.

4. I Gave Myself Permission to Disappoint People

This was the hardest one. I had to get comfortable with people being upset that I wasn't always available. But you know what? *Their disappointment is not my problem.* If someone is mad because I chose my peace over their convenience, that's their issue to work through, not mine.

Standing on Business Means Standing on YOU

At the end of the day, boundaries are about *self-preservation*. They're about making sure that you have enough energy left for *yourself*. Because if you keep giving and giving with no limits, you'll wake up one day completely depleted, wondering why no one is there to refill *you*.

So let this be your reminder: **It's not your job to save everyone. It's your job to save yourself first.**

- Protect your peace.

- Set your boundaries.

- Stand on business.

Because if you don't take yourself seriously, why should anyone else?

Chapter 11

"Unapologetic Energy Only"

(Confidence & Mindset Shifts)

I'm a Capricorn, so I'm opinionated by nature. And I won't lie—sometimes the things I say come out *harsh*, but let's be real... they're usually *true*. It took me a minute to learn how to say what needs to be said without it sounding so damn mean. But what I won't do? **Start sugarcoating my truth just to make other people comfortable.**

For too long, I shrank myself. I bit my tongue when I should've spoken up. I softened my words so people wouldn't call me aggressive or *too much*. But I realized something— **dimming my light never made anybody shine brighter.** If my presence, my success, or my *realness* is too much for someone, that's not my problem.

See, being unapologetic ain't about being rude or reckless—it's about standing in my truth without shrinking. It's about knowing my worth and refusing to explain myself to people who were never gonna understand me anyway.

Funny how folks love you as long as you stay in the lane *they* put you in. But the moment you start thinking bigger, moving differently, speaking bolder, they hit you with: *"You've changed."*

Damn right, I changed. I grew. I healed. I started loving myself for real. And I stopped asking for permission to exist.

So now? I walk with my head high, my energy protected, and my spirit *free*. If you're here for that, welcome. If not? Step aside.

This life is too short to be anything but **unapologetically me.**

And the same goes for you, too!

The most powerful thing you can be in this world? **Unapologetically YOU.** Too often, we water ourselves down to make people comfortable. We play small so we don't intimidate the weak. We hesitate, second-guess, or let self-doubt talk us out of our greatness. But **not anymore.**

This section is about **owning who you are**, walking into every room like you belong there (because you do), and **moving like you're unstoppable—because you ARE.** If you've ever let fear make your decisions, if you've ever worried about what people might say, or if you've ever hesitated to take up space—these affirmations will put that nonsense to bed.

Confidence is not arrogance—it's self-respect. And from now on, **you will never apologize for knowing your worth again.**

Here are a few insights that you can turn into lifelong mantras. Sometimes, we all need a little reminder.

"I am not for everyone, and that's a good thing."

You weren't meant to be liked by everybody. Stop shrinking yourself to fit.

"My presence is a privilege."

If they don't appreciate you, remove yourself. Simple.

"I am enough, just as I am."

No upgrades needed. You're already that person.

"I don't compete, I dominate."

You're not here to participate. You're here to win.

"I refuse to let fear make my decisions."

Feel the fear. Do it anyway.

Chapter 12

"Real Talk: Take This With You"

Life is gonna test you, shake you, and sometimes make you question everything—but you are *built for this*. These reminders aren't just words; they're truths to hold onto when things get tough. Read them when you feel stuck, when doubt creeps in, or when you need that extra push to keep going. Let them remind you of your power, your worth, and the greatness waiting for you on the other side of fear. No matter what life throws at you, remember: *you got this, and you're not alone.* Now, go be everything you were meant to be!

Stop Waiting for Permission to Shine.

Nobody is going to hand you the life you want. You have to step up and *take it*. Stop waiting for the perfect moment, the right circumstances, or for someone to tell you it's your time. Your time is *now*. Walk like you own it.

Growth Ain't Always Pretty, But It's Worth It.

Transformation comes with discomfort. You'll have to shed old habits, old mindsets, and sometimes even old friendships. But don't fear the process. Every version of you that had to break was making space for the one that's about to bloom.

Energy Speaks Louder Than Words.

Pay attention to how you feel around people. If someone drains you, confuses you, or disrupts your peace, that's your answer. You don't need closure, and you don't owe explanations. Move accordingly.

Happiness Is an Inside Job.

Nobody is responsible for making you happy but *you*. It's not in a relationship, a job, or material things. It's in how you speak to yourself, how you care for yourself, and what you allow into your space.

Bet on Yourself Like Your Life Depends on It.

Because it does. Every dream you have is waiting for you to believe in it enough to make it real. Stop underestimating your power. Stop letting doubt win. Go all in on *you*.

If It Costs You Your Peace, It's Too Expensive.

I don't care what it is—a relationship, a job, an opportunity. If it's keeping you up at night, if it's making you question your worth, if it's draining your spirit—it's not worth it. Walk away and don't look back.

Your Circle Should Inspire You, Not Drain You.

If you're always the one giving, checking in, and holding everybody together, It might be time to reevaluate. Surround yourself with people who pour into you just as much as you pour into them.

Your Dreams Require Action, Not Just Hope.

Manifesting is powerful, but you have to *move* too. Stop sitting on ideas. Stop making excuses. Start putting in the work, because the universe meets you at the level of your effort.

Not Everyone Deserves a Front Row Seat to Your Life.

Be mindful of who you allow in your space. Some people are only around to watch, not to support. Protect your energy and be selective with your access.

You Are Built for This.

You've survived every hard day, every setback, every storm—and you're still standing. Don't let doubt trick you into thinking you can't handle what's ahead. You are strong. You are capable. And you *will* win. **Period.**

Epilogue:
Step Into Your Power

Listen, every day isn't gonna be your best day. Some mornings, you'll wake up feeling like you can conquer the world. Other days, it might take everything in you just to get out of bed. But here's the thing—**we have the power to reshape our reality just by changing the way we think.** Our mindset controls everything. The way we see ourselves, the way we handle challenges, the way we react to setbacks—it all starts in the mind.

And the biggest key to growth? *Being willing to learn.* The moment we stop learning, we stop evolving. We might as well be dead. Life is about movement, about transformation, about *leveling up* every single day. But here's what they don't tell you—**growth changes things.** Sometimes that means the people around you won't fit in your world anymore. The bonds you thought were unbreakable start to loosen, and yeah, that shit hurts. But the truth is, *not everybody is meant to travel the whole journey with you.*

Some people were only meant for a season, and that's okay.

Your success? It ain't for everybody to share. Some people won't understand it. Some won't support it. And some? They'll resent you for it. But you gotta stay focused. **You can't keep pouring into people who don't pour back into you the way they expect you to pour into them.**

And before you can even think about giving to others, you gotta be full yourself. You can't help somebody else if you don't even have it to help *yourself*. That's why learning to say *no* is a form of self-care. **Protecting your peace, your energy, your time. That's not selfish, that's necessary.**

So, as you close this book, I hope you walk away with your head higher, your heart stronger, and your spirit ready to take on whatever comes next. Keep growing, keep pushing, and most importantly, keep choosing *you*. Because at the end of the day, **you are your own greatest investment.**

You got this, and you're not alone!